PETER M BOURRET

Snowflakes from the Other Side of the Universe

PETER M BOURRET

Snowflakes from the Other Side of the Universe

CreateSpace

Poetry / Nonfiction

First Edition (August, 2015)

First Printing (August, 2015)

ISBN-13:978-1515028840

ISBN-10-1515028844

DEDICATION

For the Honorable Judge John Roll, my friend from our days of innocence as classmates at Salpointe Catholic High School.

The truly tragic events on that 8th day of January in 2011 stole John away from so many who cared about him. Had I known that our conversation at our 45th high school reunion, several months prior to his murder, would be our last, I would have said my good-byes to him.

I take this opportunity to dedicate this book of poetry to you, my friend John. Horatio, Prince Hamlet's faithful friend, said it best: "Now cracks a noble heart. Good-night sweet prince: And flights of angels sing thee to thy rest."

CONTENTS

Acknowledgements
Preface

ACKNOWLEDGEMENTS

Although writing is a solitary venture, a number of people have helped me on this journey in a variety of ways. In addition to her support, Cheryl Watters was invaluable, helping me fine-tune my poems with her insightful observations. Numerous people have tirelessly encouraged and supported my writing efforts: my son Jeremy Bourret, Bob Kish, Megan Hughes, Sue & Chuck Peters, Liz & Michael Callahan, Carolyn Kittle, Melvin Martin, Chrystal Lynn, Forest Danford, Gretchen McFarron, Vicki & Howie Hibbs, Jeff Stensrude, Karen Schwabacher, Dr. David Beil, Dr. Otto Kausch, Robin Mirante, Steve Johnson, Wendy LaFave, Dale Witzman, Ron Whiteman, Mike Fitz, Don Harmon, Jim Chard, Steven Bates, Pepper Pro, the Brewers: Mike, Lydia, Ryan & Heather, Mary Langer Thompson, Ron Cecchetti, Phil Tully, John Lynch, Pat DeVito, Eva Lang, Mark Chandler, Michaele Chapman, Kay Sullivan (President of Salpointe Catholic High School) and Danetta Mecikalski, Rudy Saldivar, Erin Fitzgerald Jacobs, Rachel Milligan, Wendy Newell, Shirley Ward, and Hilary Quick--seven of my former students. Rose Pearson, the creative director and founder of The Writers' Circle, Inc., believed in me and published *WAR: a memoir* online. Mary Pat Sullivan, Damiana Cohen, Jerry Barkan, John Sole, Lynda Gibson, Marcus Conway, Barb Noel, Morris & Sharon Barkan, and my sister Mary Bourret have been a faithful audience, always willing to listen to my poetry and to offer feedback. I would be remiss if I failed to mention my mom, a gifted writer, tireless in her support of my love of writing

I am indebted to Denham Clements, a fellow Marine and Nam vet, who not only provided the cover art (from his award-winning "Vietnam Elegy") for my previous book of poetry but has tirelessly supported my writing. Bill Black, a fellow poet and Vietnam War vet, has not only encouraged me and supported my writing, but he has been invaluable with his technical assistance. Additionally, I owe a thank-you to Dave Barger and Tina Carbo for their technical help putting together the cover. Finally, I am grateful to Barbara Beamer for creating the beautiful, watercolor artwork for my cover. If I have forgotten someone, please forgive me. This won't be my last book, so I'll make sure I'll remember for the next one.

PREFACE

Each poem I write has a life of its own, but each poem is also a stepping-stone to my next poem.

Writing is a process, so writer's block does not frustrate me because I see it as nothing more than a traffic sign guiding on the road to a poem or a chapter in a novel. If the brick wall doesn't crumble quickly, I go to another place where I will find success. *Eventually* and *faith* are the key words: the brick wall will disappear and the word, line, or idea will appear when the time is right. I go with the flow and believe that the process will take care of me.

When I write poetry, I am not concerned with finishing a poem in one sitting. I write down as much as is floating through me: a phrase, an idea, or several lines. Eventually, I go back to these tidbits and grow them, and they blossom into poems, but only when they are ready and I am ready. There have been times when I have been taking a relaxing bath and words and phrases would begin floating down like snowflakes, and I would jump out of the tub and run to my computer to type these ideas which, in one case, turned into a finished poem, one completed in a single sitting; it felt like I was the stenographer for the muse from the other side of the universe. I do not sit down at my keyboard with the intention of writing a poem, but rather I leave the window to my soul open and let the butterfly of unborn poetry enter and sit on my shoulder when it is ready. When the words to a poem arrive, I am powerless to do anything else but write. For me, writing is oxygen, and poetry is the language of the universe, and I must listen. If there is a hell, I would know that I were there if I were told on my first day there that I would not be allowed to write poetry for eternity.

I find poetry's dance to be a healing experience in the same way that intimacy keeps a relationship healthy and vibrant. Intimacy is all about being vulnerable and being willing to become visible to another person. When I write poetry, I share who I am, making myself, my soul, visible for all who read my poetry. The reader is treated to a slide show of the landscape of my journey. Aha moments, an essential element in the creation of a poem, percolate below the surface, waiting for the invisible connecting-of-the-dots process to finish; eventually, a poem is born. The process of writing poetry brings out that which must see the light of day. Writing poetry is like being in a relationship without secrets; the creative process enables me to share, to pour out my rivers of thought laced with emotion.

Although the selections of poetry in *Snowflakes from the Other Side of the Universe* might not appear to be part of the same tapestry, with a closer examination, one can recognize that *writing, being, seeing, mortality,* and *grief* are threads in the tapestry of life. And so, I share my observations and insights from my journey. Enjoy.

PROLOGUE

1. - the address of the aha moment

the perfect words for my poem
effortlessly floating down
like snowflakes
from the other side of the universe
where factories produce similes
where farms grow metaphors
where the CEO is my muse

WRITING

2. - the futility of fighting off a poem

there's no *to write or not to write*
that is the question
only my pounding on a computer keyboard
in the undemocratic world of writing

like an obedient child
I must obey the muse

like a person in AA
I'm powerless
I must write

3. - a poem is born

the road map of a poem
begins in the universal womb

its journey flows freely
strolling through the heart, hungry for healing
meandering through the mind meant for more than madness
and when the time is right
the poem is born on a field of white
now no longer barren
but ready to be harvested
by those who know
that poetry is more than metaphors
which are only ornaments hanging on a tree
poetry is the wind whistling through that tree

4. - words in search of a home

a blank wilderness
barren and painted endless white
just over the ridgeline

but I can see words on the march
like bands of hunter-gatherers
prowling the countryside

5. - a poet's unconditional love affair with a blank page

the blank sheet of paper
the playground for my words
has never walked away
or hung up the phone
because my words bumped up against it too hard

the snow white paper
only smiles
knowing that someone bothered to sprinkle
words
sometimes lyrical
sometimes sad and filled with ancient pain
these words
all citizens of the heart
beg to be heard
by that true inner ear
that listens beyond the letters that huddle together
becoming words and phrases

6. - when nouns fail us and verbs are our salvation

my net is always out
as I wait patiently for a school of ideas
to swim in from the Jungian ocean
while
the Buddha sits
on a wave
on the shore
on a cloud
on a rain drop
smiling

7. - the flight of a poem

floating freely
flapping fragile wings
in the afternoon air outside my window
a butterfly

if I want it to sit on my shoulder
I must first open the window
letting in both the warm breeze
and the butterfly
maybe I'll be its airport
or maybe it will fly away

a poem floating in from the other side of the universe
is like a fickle butterfly
it will land when it is ready
some poems are ready for birth
for the cutting of the umbilical cord
but sometimes the labor pains must continue
a poem will eventually land
    if I open
        the window to my soul
        the universal soul

8. - the pilgrim's alphabet

we all travel from point A to point B
often on a circuitous road
sometimes it's a serpentine super highway
but usually we stumble along
on a winding and bumpy back road cloaked in fog
and the geometry of the journey knows
no right angles
no straight lines proud of their perfection
geometry and geography surrender
to the existential alphabet
where we reach into that pile of letters tossed in front of us
picking one and then another
adding our own letters
which become the words
the sentences
the paragraphs
the chapters
that make up our memoir

9. - the life of a poem

I

the empty sheet of white paper
is my hardwood dance floor
where my words
roam rhythmically
and my laughter
is the child of my insight
and my joy is the space
between the lines of my poetry

II

when the snowflakes finally fall
like paratroopers over Normandy
when each piece in the puzzle that is a poem
gathers together like a snowy Christmas countryside
when the trip from the other side of the universe
only needs a final punctuation mark
the poem peers up from the page
smiling
waiting to be shared

III

but sometimes shadows lurk
a poem unread
a poem never heard
is like an unopened bottle of the best Bordeaux
fine French wine remaining corked
and never tasted
only waiting

10. - a literary hero

Shakespeare never pondered the question:
to write or not to write
he was blind to the brick wall of writer's block
a stranger to his literary lexicon
he smelled an idea in the air
like a wildebeest at the watering hole
his eyes saw
and his ears heard
the endless struggles
and the foolish follies
practiced daily
by the beast pretending
to be a king
but instead was a court jester to the bone

only the brave venture to the watering hole
where the Bard bathed and drank
it will never dry up
of ideas that blossom
but
there is a lion waiting in the wings

11. - the genuine GPS

my North Star
my magnet marinated in wisdom
hangs out on the other side of the universe
its pipeline flowing faithfully and freely
filling my head
filling my heart
I never worry about running on empty
my to-do list is strictly for entertainment
my to-*be* list always shows up
holding hands with a poem

12. - happily helpless

the words to a poem show up
always unannounced
impatiently pounding on the door
not even wasting their time ringing the doorbell
and even before I can answer the door
a gang of words busts it down or picks the lock
and strolls in resolutely
roaming at will
confident
that I won't exercise my Second Amendment right
to shoot intruders because they know
I don't shoot metaphors in the head
I relish them
and invite these invaders
to share a beer
and tell their story

I am their prisoner
drenched in the Stockholm syndrome
as I smile broadly

13. - letters longing for meaning

emaciated words
like a once-proud mine shaft
now empty and filled with a black silence
no more riches lurking
just a black hole
the insignificant West Virginian kind
that would only bring a yawn
from Stephen Hawking

words are more than a family of letters
and when the river of emotion is damned up
like a TVA project built around the heart,
words will die

on the side of a dead-end road
meaning will perch in a dying tree
staring
waiting to fall off the branch
useless

14. – patience and the art of not fishing in the ocean of ideas

like a ship's broad fishnet
pain snares the similes and the metaphors
floating in the ocean of ideas
capturing them
mocking the village fisherman
who's on the wrong side of the net

these words will wait
while the fisherman
returns to the shore
in his empty skiff
but he smiles

tomorrow's horizon awaits
and the ocean currents will guide him
to that perfect place to cast his net
where the fish await their fate

BEING

15. - the gentle whisper

like a naked sheet of paper
waiting for Mozart to ink the perfect notes
the wind chime waits patiently
for an afternoon breeze
to bring its rhythm
so God can pen a single symphony
never to be heard again
unless I close my eyes
and swim in the river of remembrance

16. - the 20-20 vision of the heart

the blind man staring at the Mona Lisa
sees no smile
and the sunset, taken for granted by so many,
is a missing piece in his sightless puzzle
he drowns in hopeless wonder
about shapes and colors
those elusive alien objects
like ghosts
floating through the black landscape
    a nocturnal forever
where imagination is only a polysyllabic word
made useless by his blind birth
so, with stoic zeal
and with the eyes of an artist
    he sees
        the stars laughing
        the clouds crying
        the sunsets smiling
the blind man beaming
as he smiles
    with his eyes
    with his heart
        the windows to his sighted soul

17. - the obsolescence of cardboard characters

in the novel of one's life
the words tell the story
but the punctuation marks flesh it out
those blips in the narrative
paint the deeper picture
whether as the blemishes of a good man
or as the incidental acts of kindness of an evil man
the narrative is never a run-on sentence
the meal always has a dash of salt and pepper

18. - the grammar of being

I've written thousands of words
but I'm not a writer
I've loved passionately
but I'm not a lover
I've killed those trying to kill me
but I'm not a killer
I've taught thousands of children
but I'm not a teacher
I've thought millions of thoughts
but I'm not a thinker
I've learned a lifetime of lessons
but I'm not a learner
I've lived in the present moment
but I'm not a Buddhist
I've existed
but I'm not an existentialist

and I wonder
when a cloud
stops being a cloud
and becomes rain
and when rain
becomes a river
and when a river
becomes an ocean
and when an ocean
becomes a cloud

when will I stop juggling nouns and verbs in the air
when will I stop worshiping at Webster's church
when will I step outside and feel the sun on my skin
when will I be two or three again
surrendering to silly
dancing around a clock with hands stuck on *now*
smiling with a child's innocent eyes
when will I just *be*

19. - passing by

while my plane was landing in a swamp called yesterday
I was dancing with past-tense verbs
thumbing through a calendar
juggling those *might-have-beens*
    those *maybes*
    those *shoulds*
meanwhile my life was passing me by

20. - journey

go outside
and you will find risk
but also
you will see the stars
or
stay at home
on the shores
of the old world
safe from the edge
of a flat world

be Columbus
or Cousteau
or an astronaut
or the darling toddler
you once were
boldly taking that first step
into success or failure
into the history book
of your life
into the new world
which isn't new
but rather
is newly discovered
by the brave soul
choosing to begin
the journey outward
the journey inward

21. - the finishing school

time
the great editor
refines us slowly
like 320-grit sand paper
but sometimes not so gently
getting our attention with 50 grit

22. - strolling across the minefield on Shakespeare's stage

lurking in the shadows
our flaws
some fatal
some painful pinpricks
wait patiently
sometimes teasing
but always testing
and defining us

23. - perfectly faded and frayed

buddhist prayer flags flapping
fluttering freely
frayed tattered threads
time travelers vaguely remembering
yesterday's bolder pinks and greens
generous hues that have surrendered to the sun
now
    only faded colors remain
now
    only memories linger
but somewhere those once fresh pastels
float effortlessly in the ether
perfectly present
somewhere
still
silent
a lighter shade of yesterday
a perfect shade of *now*

oh, to be those threads
tattered and torn
floating freely
finding
peace
just being
saying goodbye to the pretense
of being a flag

24. - being

outside my window
orange tree
obeying the wind
perfect partner
rhythmic dancing
accepting God's breath
not wondering
just being
I want to be that tree

SEEING

25. - the singing wire psalm

acrobats
    on the telephone wire
birds
    singing alleluia
    reminding me
God loves
    even the city

26. - the real rock stars

like John Muir,
geometry,
Euclid's prodigious child,
roams the Yosemite Valley
holding hands with geology
oh so promiscuous
so many sides
a supplicant
a museum bowing to geometry
oh so infinite
kissing these rocks
snuggling up
to the geology of endless
granite possibilities
oh such a marvelous math

high school geometry with
its square, its rectangle, its octagon
never met the geometry of Yosemite's geology
the multisided rocks
seducing Muir
and many more

click
my camera is in love
completely mesmerized
meanwhile
back in the Bible belt
the fundamentalists fret about the number of days
of this thing called creation
God and John Muir can only chuckle

27. - time to be

if your eyes are hungry for a magical sunrise or sunset
don't bellow at the straight-up hands on the clock
midnight is a helpless employee of Father Time
just wait
the magic will arrive
when the time is right

28. - seeing through the noise

my silence screams at me
the cicada symphony boldly blaring
this auditory irony
nothing more
than a theme for Simon and Garfunkel
and the one o'clock sun,
a compassionate Buddha eye in the western sky,
smiles warmly
the noisy silence *is*
the duck
gliding effortlessly through water *is*
the blue wall paper
pretending to be a one-o'clock sky *is*
and I *am*
one thread in this tapestry
of sound
of sight
of warmth
my smile flows through the screaming army of cicadas

29. - now

in buddhaland every day is new year's day
in the buddha time zone
the face of the clock is naked of numbers
and is tattooed with three letters
now

30. - stolen moments

carrying the groceries home,
a black ant roams randomly.
flowing with the rhythm of a warm January breeze,
a butterfly flutters freely.
standing stately,
a saguaro hands the keys for a loft apartment
to a cactus wren.
reaching into an Arizona sky,
naked mesquite branches slow-dance
with a fickle breeze.
and riding on the four-o'clock shuttle,
an almost moon sneaks over the Rincons.

I am blind to all of this
while I sit shackled
watching *yesterday* and *tomorrow*
a double feature
playing in my head
the smell of the popcorn floats by me unnoticed
and in two minutes or in three years or maybe never
I can wake up from this dream

finally
seeing
smelling
listening
tasting
touching
feeling
the ordinary

those vibrant threads
perfectly woven
in the tapestry of life

and maybe
I'll see a tabby cat wag its tail
meowing
lingering by the door
cat body language for
I have an afternoon moon to see

31. - rainy ribbons smiling

the road sign's eye-catching yellow geometry
announcing that the right lane ends
lurking behind it
the pastel ribbons of the rainbow
are smiling at five-year-olds
who practice the art
of standing on their heads
especially on rainy days
because they know something
that goes unnoticed
for the zombie drivers
on the way to the land of cul de sacs
past road signs
past low-hanging rainbows
past the cloudy canvas

these nickel-children
wise beyond their years
seeing the cotton candy that floated away
seeing the lipstick smile painted on these clouds
because they know
that up-side-down isn't always bad
especially on a rainy day

32. - the full weather report

on the road to rainbow-land
we slog through the mud and muck
a soup of sorrow and sadness
drenched in thunderstorms
and sometimes
cursing our predicament
but forgetting
that the lightning
never struck us

33. - tenacious good

below the hard bone-dry soil
a seed sits silently waiting
this victim of the drought
wrapped in an ancient memory
a Buddha lesson
taught gently by a mother
married to the earth
the seed stretches
reaching to break through the angry and stubborn surface
of the barren wasteland
cultivated so many summers ago
a green sprout raises its arms
in praise
in the sunshine

34. - no time for guilt

when the dagger is thrust into the heart
it doesn't do a credit check
nor sneak a peek at a bank account
nor run through a resumé
the heart still bleeds
the wound still must heal
and compassion is the only currency that matters
in the matters of the heart

35. - foolish or forward

diversions
oh, so delicious
but dripping in delusions
a delightful dance
a dalliance in delaying
down the road
with its potholes
speed bumps
and red lights that fall asleep
but the toll must always be paid
or the traveler will be married to a treadmill

36. - the tapestry is not a mirror

we are the tapestry
not only the threads in the tapestry
but for me to see the picture completely
I must stand back to notice
and not be tricked
into looking with Narcissus's eyes
seeing only the beauty of the individual threads
but rather to gaze with Buddha-eyes
seeing that we are more than separate strands
and in the geography of existence
we are part of John Donne's main

37. - the magic stop sign

Arizona sunsets,
be advised
there's a new kid in town
rode in on the rainstorm

an indelible rainbow
tattooed across yesterday's confederate canvas
invisible to the citizens of hustle-and-bustle-land
but a mesmerizing momentary masterpiece
savored by those seduced
and babbling in Roget's adjectives
about this moving spectacle

the lingering storm
the low-hanging clouds
the loitering cold
this winter-weather road show
has packed up and left town
like a traveling circus
laced with misdemeanors
just movin' on
to the next town
the next audience
and this weather circus
with its rainbow
is now seared in my memory
in a thousand memories

it snuck into town to say *hello*
seducing
mesmerizing
this unexpected moment
the best kind of magic

...if
I allow myself to open the window
inviting in the ribbons of the rainbow
absorbing each breath
letting it all in
even the grandfather clouds
that sing back-up
to the main attraction

38. - punctuation marks in the sky

like the eyes of a new love
the afternoon clouds are magnets
impossible to escape
seductive in their simplicity
drifting away
hovering like sheep's wool
hitching a ride out of town

39. - journey traffic

life is a workshop
weird, wacky, wicked and wonderful

all travelers stroll the streets
sometimes choked with traffic going nowhere
sometimes filled with meandering souls
in search of high-octane heaven
sometimes the streets are pot-holed cul du sacs
without a view
all teeming with Shakespeare's players
most bowing to the fool's magic
absolutely certain
it will be real
this time

40. - all no-hitters are not the same

what's everyone fretting about?
creation in seven days
or maybe with a wink
what's it matter
it's just a numbers game
a smoke screen
missing the point
has anyone noticed
the artistic symmetry of nature
the perfect petal produced
without a blueprint
or an engineer
but engineers and the architects,
the masters of geometric symmetry,
will wail
pointing proudly to their masterpieces
the Eiffel Tower
the pyramids
the Empire State Building
an endless list
and God smiles
knowing He needs no kudos
meanwhile
back on planet Earth
a minor league pitcher throws a no-hitter
and is quite impressed with himself
next year he owns a losing record
in the big leagues

41. - thank God for flowers

even in the harsh desert
flowers smile at us
as they sway
dancing with the warm wind
God's breath whispering
as we stumble along on the journey
to find the next watering hole

42. - the physics of the journey

the journey of discovery is obese with irony
the fuel for this journey drops in
and these perfect pieces for the puzzle
float in like parachute supply drops at Khe Sanh
it's not about going anywhere
to find something
a truth and its perfect magic
it's not a linear exercise
point A to point B
rather
there's an ebb and flow
a perfect dance
that pieces together the puzzle
the enlightenment
the aha moments that move us
not so much one step further physically
but rather stir us
in our hearts
in the depths of our souls
and so we see
with a hungry Harris's hawk's eyes
the sunrise's hello
the sunset's good-bye
the jet black night
with new eyes
knowing that sunrises and sunsets are just bookends
for a night sky
that is cloaked in darkness
an ironic gift
so we can see the sparkle of the stars

43. - mirror image

Dracula avoids a mirror
Narcissus covets a mirror
such foolish folly

44. - unholy Halloween mask

when you dance with evil
it always dresses up
sporting the finest clothes
smelling so good
strutting with confidence
Marilyn Monroe sexy
or Clark Gable handsome
the perfect costume for the sales pitch
never the costume of a nursery-rhyme witch
no wrinkles
no scraggly hair

dance with evil
you can pretend
that the skunk juice wasn't sprayed
but when you sleep
it will seep into your soul
ask Lady Macbeth
about hand soap

45. - OM

the Buddha chased enlightenment
an elusive butterfly
always out of reach
because he was reaching
then
he sat down
under a banyan tree
stopping his search
for that magic something
now breathing in
now letting go
continuing to breathe
rhythmically
like ocean waves rolling through new lungs
and with this cleansing cadence
desire for enlightenment evaporated
a cool afternoon breeze
brushing across the Buddha's face
the sun sparkling in new eyes
silent
and
alive

MORTALITY SAYS HELLO

46. - the date written with God's invisible ink

meandering mortality moments
like uninvited guests dropping in to say *hello*
so I wax philosophical
pondering
wearing the Sartre mask
I crawl under the skin of Rodin's *Thinker*
as I watch mortality do its trademark stare-down
on the road to the inevitable
where *if* is a word executed long ago
and the word *when* struts with the keys to the city
Hamlet's soliloquy sings to the sinews of my soul
the sands of the hourglass evaporate
as we know they will
but we pretend
that the sand loves to procrastinate
and disobey the law of gravity
that it will pour forever
oh, forever
beats eternity playing the role of a dead soul
unless of course
the myths are right
and the kingdom in the clouds
nirvana-land behind those pearly gates really exists
just maybe
Saint Peter hangs out at the entrance booth
surrounded by seraphim and cherubim
angels galore
flapping their wings wildly in the celestial sanctuary
cloud country
reverberating with Handel's Hallelujah Chorus

but meanwhile back on planet earth
mortality still swaggers
arrogantly in my face
knowing it packs the winning hand
because
eventually always shows up
and the Casino always wins

mortality uses no pedantic prose
no prosaic poetry
no oratorical flourish
no erudite announcement
no swaggering gait across Shakespeare's stage
clutching Yorick's skull
just to make a point
mortality only needs to knock on the door
and I am awake

so
with no apologies
for a less than subtle approach
mortality is just a mobster clutching my throat
and banging on the windows to my soul
just to make sure I'm home
before it burglarizes my complacency
then strolls through my house made of cards
glued together by my assumptions
and my delusional adolescent invincibility
perfect body armor for the land of loud noises
and casual killing shrapnel
but not for a gray-haired grandfather

so
kicking Emily Post to the ground
and stepping on my toes
and bellowing in my face,
now etched with the ravines of time,
mortality
reeks with a palpable pungent odor of a truth
worse than rotting garlic breath
reminding me that I'm no Greek god
and it's rather clear
immortality is just a word parked in Webster's book
as irrelevant as any
on a fourth-grade spelling list

47. - doing time at the VA hospital

tip-toeing backstage
at death's world-tour concert
I roam
rubbing shoulders with special John-Donne guests
and roadies and groupies galore
the family of diseases
such a lengthy litany
many married to decisions
often poorly made
all the pieces in the puzzle of that face
that twilight
before surrendering to the serenity
of the simple single sound
of subtle
sublime
silence

48. - second chances

in the land of *maybes*
the surgeon's knife
turns the hourglass over
eternity is no longer around the bend
it is in session
but
I awaken from the dream
my hourglass is filled with a California beach
and I smile up at the blue San Diego sky

49. - reality

Is this a dream?
the surgeon knife flicking off one switch
flicking on another
questions buzz around like pesky gnats
was the ICU a plane ride to my purgatory?
did my unready mind bring along my friends
as a supporting cast
like comfort food
or a child's favorite blankie?
I have
imagination
memory
reality
a multiple-choice quandary
always the Danish dilemma
a Hamlet moment

50. - cutting to the heart of the matter

at the end of a surgeon's knife
my pilgrimage will take me to the land of letting go
where acceptance is the currency

at this Buddha festival
in the *now* time zone
I will float in silence
like a helpless leaf
torn from the familiar
a tree rooted in assumptions
the wind will play with me
and drop me where it will
as a perfect piece
in the puzzle
as a chapter
or
as a final simple sentence
a single word
Yes!
punctuated with an exclamation mark

51. - getting to the heart of the matter

the nurse told me that she heard my new heart valve
said it had a beautiful ticking sound

ah, the perfect rhythm of a Swiss watch
like the lines of my poems
the cadence of my soul
reaching out to be heard
and
like the tree falling in those existential woods
I wonder
if a heart valve ticked
and no one ever heard it
would it matter?

52. - meditation on breathing

labored breathing
now magically morphing into a wallpaper design
visually soft
yet staring me down
from the stone brown place on the pallet
gasping at the pump
hungry for fuel
only finding fumes
delicious
and taken for granted
like a best friend
or a Yellowstone geyser
or thank-you cards often forgotten
but nightmare-land
where
truth serum is guzzled by all
and our demons and our terror
are water-boarded
making them speakers of the truth
where perjury is a capital crime
and the liar stands as naked as a young buck
staring east across the flatness of a Kansas field
doomed to a final fate
at the other end of a farmer's soft trigger squeeze
final forever endless and true
back in dreamland
the wallpaper bends and sways
with the unsteady rhythm of my breathing

53. - threading

Siddhartha
sitting in silence
by my side
smiling
as he weaves a thread
into the tapestry
I am that thread
for a moment

54. - letting go is so hard to do until I do it

if this be the final firefight,
as the Beatles said,
let it be
but there'll be no shrapnel
no bullets racing through the hot summer afternoon
nor the jet-back blanket of night
just that same silence
between now and then
in Limbo
the land of letting go
and my GPS keeps screaming
for me to let go of expectations

tasting
each
delicious
breath

55. - that moment

in a sterile hospital
her mother floats in the balance
life and death are dressed in capital letters
they stopped being nouns when she got the call
the news every child dreads
and she tells me that she's thankful that I care
believing that I'm so kind

how sad that she thinks I'm special
I remember when special was ordinary
and I hunger for yesterday
but I know it was killed on the highway
around the bend from the place we call *now*

56. - affluence

this benevolent blizzard of genuine gifts
friends showing their love

once again
a second chance
this time at the end of a surgeon's knife
what more could a man want

57. - realization

a hospital stay
the closest thing to being at my own funeral
like an observer
awake and aware
listening to friends
both old and new
sharing the meaning of our friendship
I'm glad I didn't have to wait to be eulogized
to savor the richness of the gift of friendship
but in the eternal landscape
the dead are limited to listening
thank yous are not on the menu
but the fortunate living
can see and feel the love grown over the years
each gentle act of acceptance
nurtured slowly
like a fragile potted plant
and so each day
one friend or another
gifts from God
saturate my soil with the water of caring kindness
I know I'm blessed
as the warm August air hugs me

58. - rehab on the street

Saturday therapy
isn't just a leisurely stroll to the end of the street
with each measured footstep
pain surges through my back
left right left
tortoise cadence
a brisk walk a month ago
but now
there's no second nature
in each intentional and slow step

exhausted
my mind fades away from this sidewalk journey
as I'm stumbling
the last few miles on my Rincon Mountain path
back when death
like a herd of drooling jackals
shadowed me
in delicious anticipation
for that moment
when I'd stumble
and drop to my aching knees
surrendering
to the inevitable
becoming their main course

59. - limitations

time is a kleptomaniac
a sometimes subtle thief,
stealing youth
stealing breaths
and finally
stealing heart beats
but never able to rob the wisdom won

60. - leaving the station on that sweet chariot ride home

fate, the playwright,
is feverishly scribbling the lines of the fifth act
        of your play
and soon you will be placed on the shelf
        in the library of life
and maybe you'll be fortunate
to have your own Horatio
to offer a good-night eulogy
and ask *'flights of angels to sing you to your rest'*
or maybe you'll just fall into eternal sleep alone
no fanfare
only one last breath and forever silence

GRIEF

61. - shades of blue

all tears trickle from the eyes
but there are those tears
that flow from the headwaters
deeper than the heart
from that spring
buried in the soul

my sadness
awakens from the coma of denial
riding this river
flowing to the sea
a soup of yesterday's sorrows
for both beggar and king

my mouth is a coat hanger
my ancient and buried sadness
leans out the window
wondering whether or not to jump
and a four-year-old boy with a frown
runs across the stage and stands on his head
and I see a smile
it's Hamlet-soliloquy time
and everyday
there's an election that matters

62. - Sorrow's Lonely Dance

Quietly, gently
I'm told you are gone,
gone forever,
but the word *forever*
explodes in my innocent ears;
with silent sad eyes,
hollow eyes
staring nowhere yet everywhere,
desperately picturing the yesterday-you,
but seeing only a portrait hung in the haze;
your face shrouded with the fog of my disbelief,
I'm certain it's only a dream,
a nightmare for me;
I hate the crowds
with their everyday chatter;
I'm alone with my bankrupt heart,
so I wheel and deal with God,
but He's in the clouds
and I'm a prisoner in my cell of loneliness,
a guilty survivor,
doing time for taking you for granted;
my stomach pays the price,
sleep evaporates from the dictionary of my life;
the warden laughs from
as he throws away the key to my cell;
the morning comes without a sunrise,
so I scream,
pounding the granite walls of my prison cell.

You are gone,
but I have this forever mortgage
on my solitary confinement;
the litany of my rage
rambles on for hours;
but my heart is in another time zone,
where hours are eternity;
pain roars out of my wounded heart
until finally I see a magical rainbow
through the mist in my eyes,
those once-upon-a-time hollow eyes;
the huge oak door of my dungeon creaks open;
my sentence is punctuated with a question mark,
this sentence of sorrow and sadness is over,
yet all I have are memories,
memories of yesterday;
and you are gone,
gone forever...

63. - Easter Sunday

Easter Sunday
and I'm lonely
    on this day of celebration
I ache for my family
but my life has been burglarized
    two sons detained
    a mother robbed
    a father kidnapped
I want to understand this justice
and I want the luxury of family arguments
    and pot roast on Easter Sunday
but I must deal with
    custody
    a graveyard
    a nursing home
There is a whisper
You bring me back from the dead also
so I play the Easter Bunny for my sons
pick wild flowers for a special mother's grave
watch a brave father dying too slow a death,
    teaching a slow son lessons

64. - weather to grieve

the sky
a dead canvas
with lead clouds hanging precariously
and I hope they defy gravity
a mist of acid rain floats through
the stagnant air in search of a home
a resting place
my heart is heavier
than those hovering clouds
and my tears still remain home
disobeying Newton and his law
maybe the weatherman will predict rain soon
refreshing the stifling air
with a special freshness
a mourning mist

65. - temper tantrums in the land of grief

I kick and scream
as I stare at the puzzle pieces dumped in front of me
ah, the edge pieces
such an easy starting point
but they are nowhere to be found
a cruel joke
every piece is black
a Kentucky-coal-mine puzzle
without a canary
how befitting
just the hodgepodge of random shapes
like five hundred states
in a country called confusion
so I scream for some justice
whining, wondering what I've done to deserve this
and staring up at me
the pieces
five hundred too many
collecting dust
listening to the rhythm of the grandfather clock
its monolog
tick tock
the afternoon sky melts away
surrendering to the coal-colored canvas called night
and the pieces of the puzzle still gawk
as they wait nonchalantly
quadriplegics listening and staring
at a man with free hands
empty hands
waiting impatiently
waiting for the magic
of a matchmaker for these puzzle pieces

but still staring
the jigsaw family waits
as tiny bits of dust float in silence
like snowflakes on a quiet December night
falling freely
magically becoming a snowman
but this puzzle is in the desert
waiting

EPILOGUE

66. - The Long Road to Twenty-twenty Vision

I browsed through a lifetime of your poetry,
and discovering the poem that you wrote
in the days before you left,
I was hijacked by tears
before I could finish the meal of your words.
You were a mother telling the world,
telling a son that she didn't want immortality
but only the chance to share.

I was a younger man when you left,
and at this moment I ache for the chance
to share the newly discovered joy in my life.
You only wanted others to see the beauty
in small things,
and slowly I am beginning to see the beauty
that the camera of your mind
caught so many years ago.
You spoke of the strength of life
in the roots underfoot,
twisting through the earth,
and today I realize that those roots are you.
But you weren't looking for immortality,
yet your words from a thousand yesterdays ago
touch the heart of a son
who wishes he were four years old
and his mother were hugging him
because a little boy needs a gentle hug
on a stormy Ohio night.
Now it is a calm January day in the Arizona desert,
and the woman, who only wanted to share,
lives in her son's heart.

INDEX BY FIRST LINE
First Line　　　　*Poem Number*

ABOUT THE AUTHOR

Born in New York City, Peter M. Bourret, a proud grandfather and father of two sons, has lived in Tucson, Arizona for over sixty years, where he attended twelve years of Catholic school, graduating from Salpointe Catholic in 1965. After he served with the 1st Battalion, 7th Marine Regiment, 1st Marine Division as an 81mm mortarman in Vietnam during 1967 and 1968, he studied at the University of Arizona, graduating in 1971 and received a Masters Degree from the U of A in 1974. During college, he volunteered with an adult education program for several years and taught in Tucson for his entire teaching career: social studies for seven years at Apollo Middle School; then, he taught English for eighteen years, seventeen at Sahuaro High School. The author of several hundred poems, Bourret has also written a soon-to-be-published novel. He was the subject of *Strands of Barbed Wire,* a documentary about his PTSD and his return trip to Vietnam in 1991; he also participated in *Vietnam Across America*, a documentary, produced by his son Jeremy Bourret, which examines PTSD and its legacy with Vietnam War combat veterans and their families. He was a candidate for the school board in Tucson in 1976 and is an avid hiker, who has traveled extensively, including two return-trips to Vietnam. During the Bosnian War in 1993, he brought humanitarian aid to Bosnian refugees.

During his retirement, Bourret has volunteered in the local public schools, teaching writing to second and tenth graders; he also has supported a school in Nicaragua with books; currently, he volunteers at the VA, teaching classes to veterans who are experiencing PTSD symptoms. Additionally, he teaches classes about PTSD to nursing students at the VA. He has been a hospice volunteer, focusing on the veteran population. He also has been a guest speaker on the topic of the Vietnam War and PTSD in local high schools for the past twenty-five years; furthermore, he has presented poetry readings in local high schools and libraries, and most recently to the High Desert Branch, California Writers Club. Bourret is a charter member of Detachment 1344 of the Marine Corps League and is a life member of Vietnam Veterans of America. In July 2015, the author received a 1st place award for a prose piece titled "Perspective" from the VA National Creative Arts Festival and has been invited to attend the Festival in Durham, N.C. Last year, he received 1st place in the United States for "Alone with *it* on Veterans Day" in the personal experience category and was asked to present his prize-winning piece at the 2014 VA National Creative Arts Festival in Milwaukee. *War: a memoir,* which deals with his PTSD, was published online by The Writers' Circle, Inc. in June of 2014. *The Physics of War: Poems of War and Healing,* his first book of poetry, was published in January of 2015; and *Land of Loud Noises and Vacant Stares*, his second book of poetry, was published in March of 2015. Although he has written extensively about war and its consequences, *Snowflakes from the Other Side of the Universe*, his newest book of poetry, deals with aspects of the author's perspective on life. Currently retired, Bourret is in the process of writing his memoir.

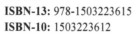

Old Eyes, Grey Souls By Bill Black

Veterans are often heard to say "You wouldn't understand, you haven't been there." What are these images and memories that can be so misunderstood? Through poems that explore a veteran's soul, you are shown what these veterans wish families and friends could understand. Wars have colors, smells and images which can quickly and involuntarily summoned. To remember brings pain but to forget betrays wounded and dead fellow soldiers. These small groups of tormented people shape our world even though most people never know them.

ISBN-13: 978-1500886325 **ISBN-10**: 1500886327
Regular Price: Book - $15.00

Cattlemen At The Cantina By Bill Black

Bill said, "These are collected poems from my shows and recordings of over two decades for those who want to see what the poems look like. Most have never been in print other than as a script in my pocket. I also give some notes on performing poetry shows. These poems have been edited and polished in shows and recording studios. They bring laughs, sighs, a few tears and moments you will want to share aloud. This collection is the majority of three CDs and an audio book contribution set s from 2002 to 2012."

ISBN-13: 978-1503223615
ISBN-10: 1503223612
Regular Price: Book - $16.00

For More By Peter M. Bourret Or Bill Black Go To Amazon.com

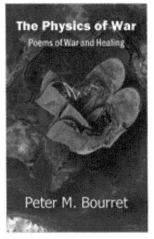

The Physics of War – Poems of War and Healing
By Peter M. Bourret
Bourret reaches deep within his personal war experience as a Marine and shares with the reader a glimpse of the true nature of war and its long term consequences. His observations and insights will profoundly impact the way the reader views war.
ISBN-10: 1502471973
ISBN-13: 978-1502471970
Price: $15.00

Land of Loud Noises and Vacant Stares
By Peter M. Bourret
Bourret shares with the reader insights about the war experience - the profound impact of war on a twenty-year-old who discovered the horrors of war, letting the reader peek behind killing's curtain. This fasten-your- seat-belt experience will show what General Sherman meant when he referred to war as Hell, a view into PTSD and its insidious nature, the impact of war on the families at home and the arduous healing process. Combat veterans will easily recognize the topics about which Bourret writes, and those who have never known the war experience will possess a better understanding of the phrase "Thank you for your service."
ISBN-10: 1507715315   **ISBN-13:** 978-1507715314
Price: $15.00

PETER M BOURRET